Folk
Instruments

Folk
Instruments

By LEE GILMORE

Illustrated by GEORGE OVERLIE

Prepared under the supervision of Robert W. Surplus

Musical Books for Young People

LERNER PUBLICATIONS COMPANY
MINNEAPOLIS, MINNESOTA

ACKNOWLEDGEMENT

The publishers wish to express their appre-
ciation to the Chester E. Groth Music Company, Minneapolis, for supplying many of
the actual instruments illustrated in the
text, and to the Zuhrah Shrine Pipe Band
for their assistance with the section on
bagpipes.

Contents

I The Fiddle and Fiddling........................ 5

II The Banjo.................................... 7

III The Guitar................................. 11

IV The Ukulele................................ 15

V The Mandolin.............................. 19

VI The Zither................................. 21

VII The Jew's Harp............................ 25

VIII The Bagpipe.............................. 27

IX The Mouth Organ.......................... 32

X The Accordion.............................. 35

XI Square Dance Bands........................ 39

The Fiddle and Fiddling

When is a violin not a violin? "That's a silly question," you may say, "a violin is always a violin." We usually think of a violin as a beautiful instrument in the symphony orchestra. But there are times when the instrument gives out a different kind of sound, as anyone knows who has ever attended a genuine old-time square dance. When you hear the call, "Grab your partners", and the music starts, you just wouldn't think of calling it a violin. It becomes a *fiddle,* and no other word will do.

When the violin first appeared in the sixteenth century, serious composers thought its sound much too harsh for their serious melodies. But it rapidly became very popular with the common people. They found it just right for their simple tunes, and for accompanying their energetic dances. The fiddle was once the instrument for the jig, the reel, the clog, or the square dance. It continues to be used that way right down to the present day. A count was made in the state of Oklahoma, which showed that the state had about three thousand fiddlers. Fiddling today is still a very popular art.

Fiddling is, of course, very different from "violining". Violining is for ballrooms and recital halls; fiddling is for country gatherings or for people who still have the love of country-living in their souls. For beautiful tone the violinist must have the most expensive instrument he can afford. This is not so for the fiddler. He can use an inexpensive violin, or even make his own. But it is not just the quality of the instrument that gives

5

fiddling its own special sound; it is *how* the fiddler plays that makes the difference. A violinist must hold his instrument under his chin just so. The fiddler holds it against his chest, or even against his waist. The violinist must learn to master his bow in a variety of motions that take years to perfect. The fiddler moves his bow in quick, short strokes that seem to dance on the strings.

Most fiddlers know at least eight traditional tunings. The violinist always tunes in one way: G-D-A-E

If you have taken violin lessons you know that there are at least seven different positions for the left hand. The fiddler rarely uses more than the first position, which makes playing much easier, of course.

The fiddler must have nimble fingers to perform his swift-moving music. The tunes he plays are like British tunes of the eighteenth century. They were brought to this country by early English settlers who made their homes in the mountains of Virginia and Kentucky. Many quaint titles still survive, such as *Moneymusk, Soldier's Joy, Blackberry Blossom, Miss MacLeod's Reel,* and *Fishers' Hornpipe.* Fiddlers have been reported who know from three to five hundred tunes. Altogether the total number of fiddle tunes is well over a thousand.

One can't help wondering what kind of tunes that merry old soul King Cole might have listened to. At any rate we know that he didn't call for violinists. Being the fun-loving old geezer he was, he must have wanted music that would make his toes tingle, which is probably why "he called for his fiddlers three".

6

The Banjo

The banjo, as we know it, was born on American soil and is considered to be America's own contribution to folk music. As with most Americans, it had its fore-fathers in other lands, but developed into a distinct American type. Its life probably began on the plantations of the Old South, where it provided a twangy background for the singing and dancing of the Negro slaves. Thomas Jefferson published a book in 1784 in which he mentions the instrument, calling it a "banger". Every minstrel show of the 1800's boasted a banjo player. It was used in the rhythm section of jazz bands until the 1930's, when it was replaced by the guitar. It continues its career today with folksinging groups, and with combos that play "Dixieland Style". Yes, the banjo is truly American—no doubt about it.

Look closely at a fine banjo and you will see that it is quite elegant. Its long neck is usually made of walnut or satinwood, the fingerboard of ebony or rosewood. The body looks very much like a tambourine without the jingles, and is covered with a skin. Banjo players call

7

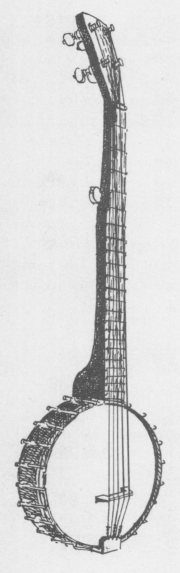

this skin *vellum*. It is really white calf skin. On a good banjo this "drumhead" is fastened in a wood or metal rim, with 24 bracket hooks. A round piece of wood is placed back of the rim and acts as a *resonator*—that is, it vibrates with the strings and makes the sound of the instrument stronger.

Many banjos have five strings. They are usually made of steel, giving the instrument its metallic sound. The strings are strummed or plucked with the right hand. We also have a four-string banjo which is played with a *plectrum* (a pick). Early players sometimes wore a metal thimble with which strings were struck, not plucked.

Normal tuning for the five-string banjo is:

The fingers of the left hand produce needed pitches by pressing the strings along the fingerboard. Finding the correct pitches is made easier, by dividing the fingerboard into sections. Raised pieces of metal called *frets* are used to divide the string into half-tones. Most folk string instruments follow the same idea.

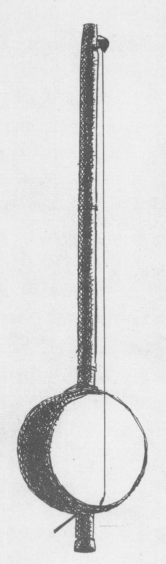

Probably the earliest known ancestor of the banjo was the *ravanastron* in India. Like the banjo it had a long wooden neck attached to a round frame over which was stretched a skin covering. The ravanastron had only one string. The closest ancestors of the banjo, however, are probably African. Instruments very much like the ravanastron have been found among primitive tribes in Africa, and it is possible that slaves brought these instruments with them. Similar instruments are known in the West Indies, where there is a large Negro population. These early instruments had from four to nine strings, though four or five was the usual number. The ravanastron and its African relatives are very ancient, and are quite crude in comparison with our modern banjo.

In the hands of an expert the banjo can produce many styles of music. One famous banjoist named Farland was able to play a sonata composed for violin by the great Johann Sebastian Bach. But if a banjo could talk it would probably tell you it is happiest making the music for which it was created — the folk music of America.

9

The Guitar

The guitar is like an actor who can play many roles. In the United States it has gained wide fame and popularity providing music for folksongs and square dancing. It is equally at home in the rhythm section of swing bands and combos, or in the beat of rock and roll. A skilled guitarist can bring forth from his instrument harp tones, reedy metallic tones, drum beats, bell sounds and tambourine effects. In the hands of a virtuoso it becomes an expressive soloist and a brilliant star in its own right.

The guitar is the largest plucked instrument in common use. The woods most commonly used for the top, back, and sides are maple, ash, or cherry. The neck and fingerboard are usually made of hardwoods such as ebony, beech, or pear. The bridge is quite often made of ebony.

The guitar has six strings, which are tuned:

Music for the instrument is written in the treble clef, but sounds an octave (8 notes) lower than written.

WRITTEN:

SOUNDS:

The fingerboard is fitted with frets or narrow strips of metal, against which the fingers are pressed to produce desired pitches.

Guitar makers very often took pride in decorating their instruments with inlaid designs of rosewood or other fine woods. Very old instruments of the seventeenth century were often inlaid with fancy designs in ivory, ebony and mother-of-pearl. Only the rich could afford such instruments. The guitar was not always the instrument of the common man; it is an instrument with a proud heritage as well.

Where and when the guitar had its origin no one knows. Some people believe that it descends from some instrument that was played with a bow, because its sides curve inward in the manner of a violin. There is no proof of this, however. It is related to the mandolin and lute of Europe, and to instruments of Asia going back thousands of years.

The tone quality of the guitar has appealed to some of the world's greatest composers and performers. Paganini, one of the greatest violinists, gave up the violin for two years, and devoted all of his time to the guitar. Verdi, a famous composer, included the guitar and the mandolin in the music for his opera *Otello*. Schubert kept a guitar beside his bed and played it before he got up in the morning. Beethoven, Berlioz, Scarlatti, and Debussy are other masters who were interested in the guitar.

In recent times jazz guitars have been developed, which are heavier and broader than the classic guitar, and have strings of steel. These instruments are played with a pick or plectrum. The jazz guitar is used mainly as a percussion instrument in swing bands and combos, although a skilled player can use it for solos. Sometimes it is amplified (made louder) electrically. Such a guitar may be much smaller and quite flat.

The Hawaiian guitar, sometimes called the steel guitar, is another variation of this instrument. It is usually tuned to an A-chord. It is held flat on the lap, and is played with picks on the thumb, index finger, and middle finger of the right hand. A bar of steel is held in the left hand and placed on the strings to produce the proper pitches. The Hawaiian guitar is especially known for its *glissando* effects. Glissando is a sliding sound produced by moving the steel bar up or down the strings while they are vibrating. This unusual effect was discovered by a Hawaiian schoolboy, named Joseph Kekuku. The story goes that he accidentally touched a knife or comb to his own guitar and was pleased with this new sound. His discovery lives on wherever steel guitars are heard.

13

The Ukulele

We think of this instrument as being a native of Hawaii; actually it is a small Portuguese guitar brought to the islands by missionaries in the late 1800's. The Hawaiians give it the name *ukulele* because of the way the fingers jump from chord to chord (*uku* meaning "insect" and *lele* meaning "jumping"). The instrument became very popular in the United States in the 1920's and is widely used to accompany campfire songs or when people sing together informally. Simple melodies can be played on the uke, but mostly it is a chording instrument.

Like the guitar the ukulele has frets on the fingerboard to help the player in placing his fingers. Each fret produces a note a half step higher than the one before. There are four strings which are tuned A - D - F-sharp - B, or

My dog has fleas.

In Hawaii, and sometimes in this country the uke is tuned G - C - E - A. With this tuning it is easier to finger chords in simple keys. Each string sounds one note lower with this system, but the tuning still sounds like "My dog has fleas".

G   C   E   A

By learning three simple chords, you can use the uke to accompany many songs. These chords are the I, the V_7, and the IV. Most school music books have them marked over the melody. The numbers come from the steps in our scale. This is how they look in the key of C.

I   IV V_7

16

You will notice that the I chord is on the first step of the scale, the IV chord on the fourth step, and the V_7 on the fifth step. Here is how they look in the key of F.

I   IV V_7

You will notice that when the bottom note of the chord is on a line, the other notes of the chord are also on lines. When the bottom note is on a space, the others are also on a space.

To help you learn to finger these chords on the ukulele, you will find on the next page a fingering chart for simple major keys. Most popular music has either fingering diagrams or chord names over the melody, and they are surprisingly easy to learn. With a little practice you could entertain your friends at a party or at school by accompanying them on "the jumping insect".

Ukulele Fingering Chart

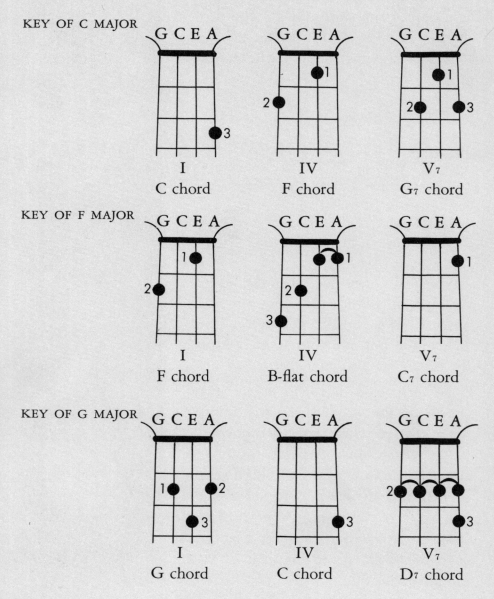

KEY OF C MAJOR

G C E A
I
C chord

G C E A
IV
F chord

G C E A
V₇
G₇ chord

KEY OF F MAJOR

G C E A
I
F chord

G C E A
IV
B-flat chord

G C E A
V₇
C₇ chord

KEY OF G MAJOR

G C E A
I
G chord

G C E A
IV
C chord

G C E A
V₇
D₇ chord

The Mandolin

Unless you live in certain areas of the United States, you may not have an opportunity to know this friendly instrument. The mandolin is not so widely used as the guitar. In spite of its thin and somewhat nasal quality its tone has something original about it that is very appealing.

The mandolin made its way to America from Spain in about 1880, but its history goes back far beyond that date. It is descended from the lute, and therefore is a distant cousin of the guitar. It is much smaller than the guitar, and its back is usually rounded rather than flat. The instrument is best suited for playing melody.

The mandolin has four double strings, two strings for each pitch. The purpose of the double stringing is to strengthen the sound. Tuning is exactly like the violin and music is written in the treble clef:

While the mandolin is mainly an instrument for folk music, great composers have written for it. We have already mentioned that Verdi included the mandolin in the music for his opera *Otello*. Mozart used it for the accompaniment of the lovely serenade in his opera *Don Giovanni*. Vivaldi, an early Italian composer, wrote music for the mandolin. Gustav Mahler is another great composer who wrote for this charming instrument.

19

The Zither

It may surprise you to learn that the zither is one of the most widely used instruments in American schools. Perhaps you have played it yourself without knowing it was a zither. You see, our old friend the autoharp is really a form of zither, with pushbuttons added to make chording easier.

The zither is a flat, shallow sound box made of wood, over which are stretched from thirty to forty strings. Four or five melody strings are nearest the player, and are stretched over a fretted finger board. These melody strings are plucked with a metal ring worn on the right thumb. The ring has a sharp spur for picking the strings. The other strings are plucked with the fingers of the left hand to produce an accompaniment. The instrument is larger than the autoharp,

21

and, of course, it has no pushbuttons.

It is believed that the zither was brought to this country by the Pennsylvania Dutch (who were not Dutch but German). It was carried southward by early settlers through the mountain regions of Pennsylvania, Maryland, Virginia, and the Carolinas. It is still in use in those sections today. Zithers of various sizes are favorites of the Bavarian and Swiss peasants, and the instrument is even played at times in the concert halls of Germany.

The zither is actually a modern version of the psaltery of Biblical times, and has a very ancient and interesting history. The psaltery is often mentioned in the Bible in connection with worship of God. For this reason it was the only instrument allowed in religious services in the early days of Christianity. In time its place in the church was taken by the organ, but it continued to be used as a folk instrument. It gradually developed into the zither which we know today.

There are zithers of different types from the one described above. Two of these are still used in sections of the U.S.A. One of them has only four strings

and is played with a bow. The tone of this instrument is not particularly pleasing, being rather harsh and nasal.

The second type is sometimes called a dulcimer. This is a simple home-made zither with three strings which are tuned

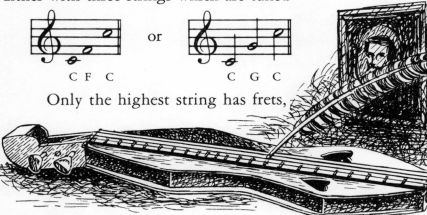

Only the highest string has frets,

which are "fingered" with a turkey quill or stick held in the left hand. A pick or a turkey quill held in the right hand sweeps across all the strings, thus producing a melody with two drones. By "drone" we mean a tone, or tones which are produced at a constant pitch while a melody is played on another string. Here is an example:

There are other dulcimers made in the mountains of the South which may have more strings. You may want to make one of the simple mountain dulcimers yourself, with which you could accompany your class when singing Appalachian folk ballads. Some of these songs are well known, such as *Barbara Allen, The Hangman's Song,* and *Little Mohee.* You may want to look up more of these old ballads. Many were brought from England by early settlers. There are still others that tell stories of the Civil War and other events in American history. Playing an accompaniment on a home made dulcimer would give these songs a real "mountain flavor".

The instrument with many strings, described first in this chapter, is the zither most commonly known. If you have enjoyed playing the autoharp, you may want to try your hand someday at playing this charming descendent of the ancient psaltery.

The Jew's Harp

How in the world did this instrument get its name? So far as we know it has no historical connection with the Jewish people. Certainly it isn't anything like a harp. Most European countries give it some form of the name *tromp* (trumpet), though it is nothing like a trumpet either. In Holland, for example, it is called the *jeudgtromp* (child's trumpet). It is probably from the Dutch that we English-speaking people have taken our name "jew's harp". Their word *jeud* (youth) is pronounced very much like the word for Jew. Some people, however, feel that the name may have really been *jaw's* harp, and it is often called that in music stores today.

By whatever name we call it, the instrument appeals to people in many parts of the world. Americans seem to like its rhythmic twang, especially when it is played in a square dance or folk band. But the jew's harp is not only for dancing. Many people find it a cheerful companion for lonesome hours, and in Austria it is known as the instrument of the lonely people.

The instrument came to America from Europe. It was brought to Europe from Asia many hundreds of years before that. A drawing made in China in the twelfth century shows it very much as we know it today. It is still used in China, where it is called *K'ou chin* (mouth harp).

The jew's harp is very simple, having only two parts. There is a metal frame in the shape of a horseshoe. The two ends extend to form arms. Between these two arms is a metal tongue which vibrates freely when set in motion by a stroke of the finger. The player holds the instrument between the front teeth in such a way that the metal tongue can move freely. Various pitches are produced by changing the shape and size of the mouth. That's all there is to it. In Asia these instruments are sometimes made of metal, but often both the frame and the tongue are made of wood. The sound of the wooden instruments is quite different from those made of metal.

Instruments resembling the jew's harp are found among primitive peoples in many parts of the world. It is interesting, however, that it was unknown to the American Indians. Certain primitive tribes in Africa make an instrument which is also played by changing the shape of the mouth. It is quite different from the jew's harp, and is known as the musical bow.

The best thing about the jew's harp is that it is so simple that everyone can play it. It is also small enough to carry in your pocket. With this friendly instrument you may have music wherever you go.

The Bagpipe

The bagpipe is an instrument that actually talks, or at least so say the Scotch and the Irish. In fact, the bagpipe is in many ways similar to the human voice. You may not be able to understand the actual words it speaks, for the Celtic people (Scotch and Irish) say they cannot be translated into English. But you don't have to be Scotch or Irish to get a thrill from this stirring instrument. To hear a bagpipe band approach as it plays *The Campbells Are Coming* can be a spine-tingling experience for anyone.

Though the bagpipe is Scotland's

27

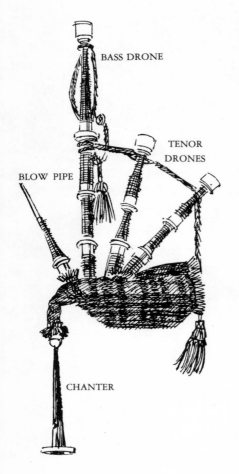

BASS DRONE

TENOR
DRONES

BLOW PIPE

CHANTER

national instrument, it is known to other countries. In Germany it is called the *dudelsack*; in France, the *musette*. It was probably played in Ireland before Scotland, but its history is older than either of these countries. It was known in Ancient Rome a hundred years before Christ, and it is said that even Nero played it. Before the bagpipe came into being, simple pipes were played at great entertainments. Sometimes two pipes were played through a single mouthpiece. In the open air it was very difficult to make the sound reach a huge audience. Sometimes a piper would blow so hard that he would break a bloodvessel. Finally one player got the idea of attaching a bag to the pipe, in which an extra supply of air could be stored. This gave the lungs a chance to rest. That is how the bagpipe was born.

Those early bagpipes were very simple. It took many years to develop into the complicated instrument we know today. The bagpipe can be best understood by looking at the picture on the left. You will see that in certain ways it resembles the instrument of the human voice.

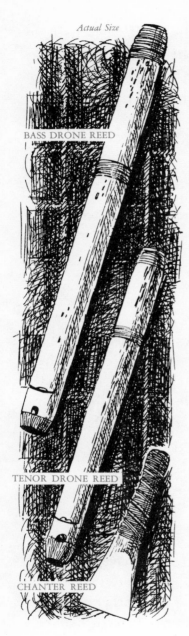

Actual Size

BASS DRONE REED

TENOR DRONE REED

CHANTER REED

The bag, which in the U.S.A. is made from an elk's skin, can be compared to the lungs. It is kept full of air by blowing into the blowpipe. The blowpipe has a gadget at the far end which keeps the air from coming back to the player. This makes it possible for the player to have a quick rest. The blowpipe does not produce sound. By pressing the bag with the elbow, air is forced through the chanter, an instrument similar to an oboe. Sound from the chanter is produced by the vibrations of a double reed (two edges of cane tied together at the base of the pipe). Notice the similarity of the double reed to the vocal cords. The piper can play melodies on the chanter by fingering the eight holes along its side. Many people believe that the chanter comes closer than any other instrument to sounding like the human voice.

Here, however, the likeness between the bagpipe and the vocal instrument ends. In addition to the chanter there are three other pipes without sound-holes. These three pipes provide an accompaniment for the chanter. They are called drones and produce one tone as long as they are supplied with air. The

29

drones are usually fitted with a single reed, somewhat like a clarinet reed.

The two short drones are about twenty inches long and sound an A.

The long drone (about three feet in length) sounds another A one octave lower.

Because the drones are constantly sounding these A's, we always seem to hear the scale of the chanter as an A-scale. However, this scale is quite different from the A-scale of the piano. The chanter can produce nine tones and is tuned as shown below.

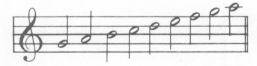

You will notice that we have written no sharp before F, C, or G. Actually these tones on a bagpipe are neither sharp nor natural, but are somewhere in between.

The sound is strange to our ears because we are used to the piano scale. The effect seems strange at first, and sounds rather oriental.

The early Celts were convinced of the talking ability of the bagpipe. They developed a bagpipe language based on their own ancient tongue. Long notes were used as vowels and grace notes as consonants. Thus melodies could be easily taught by repeating certain words or syllables. Music was handed down in this way from generation to generation.

If you ever decide to learn to play the bagpipe, remember that it is an instrument for military and very festive outdoor occasions. This instrument was first created so that thousands could hear it in a huge stadium. Perhaps you should practice alone on some distant hillside.

The Mouth Organ

Compared to other instruments discussed in this book the mouth organ, often called the harmonica, is just a youngster. It is believed to have been invented by Fredrich Buschmann of Berlin in 1821, although credit is sometimes given to Sir Charles Wheatstone in 1829. In any case it was manufactured by Wheatstone's London firm with the name *Aeolina*. Today it is one of the most widely used instruments in the world. In 1930 a German company manufactured 46 million mouth organs—enough to supply about one-fourth of the people in the United States.

The instrument consists of a small flat box a few inches long, with a number of openings along one side. Each opening leads to a metal "free" reed inside the box. A free reed is one which is fixed into a metal plate and vibrates through a slot, from one side of the plate to the other.

The harmonica is played by blowing in or out and by moving right or left in order to sound the notes. By blowing into a hole, a single note is played; by drawing air through the same hole, the next note of the scale is sounded. By playing through two adjoining holes, tones a third apart may be sounded.

IN   OUT   IN   OUT

The mouth will cover three or four holes, and those not needed must be closed with the tongue.

The harmonica is one of the easiest instruments to learn. It brings joy to millions of people who would never think of trying a more difficult instrument. It is possible to play very difficult music on the harmonica. This requires talent and many hours of practice. Larry Adler is one man who made his career on the concert stage playing the harmonica.

Between 1914 and 1918 more harmonicas went to war than any other instrument in history. The musicians of Great Britain raised a huge sum of money so that every British soldier in World War I might have his own mouth organ. The German army made use of the instrument, too. We can imagine how it helped to cheer the weary and lonely men during that great struggle.

Thousands of people have found it great fun to play in a harmonica band. The instrument is made in many sizes and ranges, and in a mouth-organ band the larger instrument can be used for playing in the lower ranges; the smaller ones, in the higher ranges. A very good effect can be had with all members playing instruments of the same size. If you do not have such a band in your school, you may want to help organize one. You're sure to enjoy it.

33

The Accordion

We need no formal introduction to the accordion; it is an old friend that is likely to greet us wherever we go. In a trailer camp in California or on a cruise to Bermuda, in Paris or New York, at a Texas barbecue or an Austrian coffee *klatsch* — in such a wide variety of places the familiar sound of this instrument can be heard. Credit for the invention of the instrument is sometimes given to Damian of Vienna, in 1829; sometimes, to Buschmann of Berlin, in 1822. Today, more than one hundred years later, it outsells all other instruments in the world, except for the mouth organ.

The sound of an accordion is produced by free reeds. The reeds are vibrated by wind supplied from a bellows. One set of reeds is used when the bellows moves out; an entirely different set, when it moves in. Both sets produce the same pitches.

The instrument is made so that it can be held in both hands. The right hand plays melody on a keyboard like that of a small piano. This keyboard has its own reeds and a range of three and one-third octaves. The left hand works the bellows and plays an accompaniment on a button board.

There are six rows of buttons on the standard 120 bass accordion. The first two rows nearest the bellows control forty bass notes which sound in octaves. The other four rows play eighty different chords, one complete chord to a button. With these bass notes and chords it is possible to harmonize melodies in any key.

Every tone in every chord has its own reed. This means that reeds for a given tone must be duplicated many times in the instrument. The standard 120 bass accordion has 448 reeds made of Swedish blue steel. This is an astonishing number for so small an instrument. Yet, if you experimented with a buttonboard, you would find that your fingers have to move very little to find the various chords in a given key. Chord arrangements for the buttonboard are shown in a chart at the end of this chapter.

Modern standard accordions have tabs above the keyboard. By moving these tabs the player can produce many different tone colors. This feature adds greatly to the variety and appeal of the instrument.

The accordion sounds best when it is playing chords with a melody. The player must therefore have a very good sense of harmony, and be able to hear chords for every melody. He must also take care to operate the bellows very smoothly to keep the wind flowing evenly. The player should make as short a pause as possible at the point where the bellows stops moving out and starts moving in.

6TH ROW
5TH ROW
4TH ROW
3RD ROW
2ND ROW
1ST ROW

1ST ROW COUNTER BASSES	4TH ROW MINOR CHORDS
2ND ROW FUNDAMENTAL BASSES	5TH ROW DOMINANT 7TH CHORDS
3RD ROW MAJOR CHORDS	6TH ROW DIMINISHED 7TH CHORDS

Chord Chart for Buttonboard

ROW 3

(a) Buttons in this row play major triads, chords with three tones, such as:  do-mi-sol (key of F).

(b) By pressing all the buttons in the third row, these triads can be played:

C   D♭   D   E♭   E   F   F♯   G   A♭   A   B♭   B

Notice that some of these triads are turned upside down (inverted). For example, the C-chord sounds G-C-E (sol-do-mi) rather than C-E-G (do-mi-sol). The reason for this inversion is that F is the lowest chord note built into the reeds. Only the triads on F, F-sharp, G, A-flat and A are in their original do-mi-sol position.

37

ROW 4

The fourth row of buttons plays minor triads. In minor triads the middle tone is a half-step lower than in major triads:

F minor   F major

ROW 5

The fifth row of buttons produces dominant seventh chords (V_7 chords). Compare the dominant seventh chord with a triad:

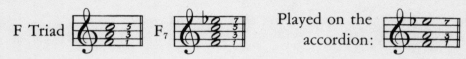

F Triad F_7 Played on the accordion:

Notice that in the V_7 chord an extra note has been added to the triad. This number 7 tone is always lowered a half step. This chord sounds well without number 5, which is left out on the accordion.

ROW 6

The sixth row produces diminished 7th chords:

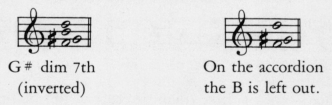

G # dim 7th   On the accordion
(inverted)   the B is left out.

Square Dance Bands

We have seen how folk instruments have come to us from all parts of the world. These instruments join together in a musical group called the square dance band or orchestra.

The make-up of these bands varies from one place to another. One instrument, however, you will hear in almost every square dance band, and that is the fiddle. This is the instrument that gives the band its square-dance sound. Generally the fiddle will be accompanied by banjo or guitar, and other instruments may be added if the players can be found. It is not at all uncommon to hear the mandolin, the jew's harp, or the mouth organ playing along with the fiddle and guitar. Sometimes a piano is used, mainly as a chording instrument. Some square dance bands even use drums. The accordion and the double bass (bass fiddle) are widely used also. You can see that there is no hard and fast rule for the organization of a square dance band.

The tune is played by the melody instruments, such as the fiddle and the mouth organ. A background of chords and a steady beat are filled in by other instruments, such as the guitar, accordion, and drums. The harmony is usually quite simple, being made up mainly of the I, IV, and V_7 chords, with occasionally perhaps a II_7 chord.

I II_7 IV V_7

Notice the sharp in the II_7 chord. This must be added to give the chord a major chord sound. If the sharp was not added, the chord would be minor.

The bass fiddle parts are often very interesting. A talented player will usually improvise or make up his part as he goes along.

Square dance bands play anywhere from five to thirty minutes at a stretch before taking a break. The music is generally loud, in order to rise above the sound of the dancers' feet and the caller's voice. And one thing you will notice—the players always seem to enjoy their work. Perhaps it is because the music they play is so filled with the simple joy of living.

A Word in Closing

Simple and familiar as some of the instruments included in this book may be, they have all been created out of man's need to express his moods and feelings, and to bring greater joy into his life. Most people take these instruments for granted, never realizing that they have such an interesting history and long tradition behind them. We hope that you have gained a better understanding by reading our book. Better yet, we hope that you have been inspired to take up one or more of these instruments yourself. No greater satisfaction can be found in life than in making music.

ABOUT THE AUTHOR

Lee Gilmore brings a wide and varied experience to the field of music education. He is a singer of great versatility, having distinguished himself across the country not only as an interpreter of folk and popular music, but in the fields of concert and opera as well. Along with his purely musical activities he has made a career as a writer, with scripts for Singer Sewing Machine, Maxwell House Coffee, and many others among his credits. Mr. Gilmore is a graduate of Teachers College, Columbia University, where he earned the Bachelor of Science and Master of Arts degrees. At present a teacher in the public schools, he is in constant contact with young people. In addition to his teaching, he is choir director at the First Presbyterian Church, Mount Kisco, New York, where he resides with his charming wife, Ilse.

NOTEWORTHY BOOKS

MUSICAL BOOKS
FOR
YOUNG PEOPLE

THE ALPHABET OF MUSIC
THE BEAT OF THE DRUM
FOLK INSTRUMENTS
FOLLOW THE LEADER [Story of Conducting]
THE HEART OF THE ORCHESTRA [Story of Strings]
KEYBOARD INSTRUMENTS
PLACES OF MUSICAL FAME
PLAYBACK: THE STORY OF RECORDING DEVICES
SHINING BRASS [Story of Trumpet and Brass]
THE STORY OF MUSICAL NOTES
THE STORY OF MUSICAL ORGANIZATIONS
THE WOODWINDS

MEDICAL BOOKS
FOR CHILDREN AND
YOUNG PEOPLE

DEAR LITTLE MUMPS CHILD
DENTISTS' TOOLS
DOCTORS' TOOLS
FUR, FEATHERS, HAIR
HOW WE HEAR [Story of Hearing]
KAREN GETS A FEVER
LEFTY [Story of Left-Handedness]
MICHAEL GETS THE MEASLES
PENNY THE MEDICINE MAKER [Story of Penicillin]
PETER GETS THE CHICKENPOX
RED MAN, WHITE MAN, AFRICAN CHIEF
    [Story of Skin Color]
THEY WOULDN'T QUIT [Story of Handicapped]
TWINS [Story of Twins]
WHY GLASSES? [Story of Vision]

MR. BUMBA BOOKS
[Easy Reading]

MR. BUMBA'S NEW HOME
MR. BUMBA PLANTS A GARDEN
MR. BUMBA KEEPS HOUSE
MR. BUMBA AND THE ORANGE GROVE
MR. BUMBA'S NEW JOB
MR. BUMBA HAS A PARTY

The above books are written by competent authorities and attractively illustrated. Information about obtaining these is available from

Lerner Publications Company

133 FIRST AVENUE NORTH
MINNEAPOLIS 1, MINNESOTA

DATE DUE

JAN 27 '65	FEB 09 1995	
5'65	MAY 09 1997	
SEP 15'65	FEB 22 2005	
OCT 6'65		
NOV 15 '67		
JAN 22 '69		
MAR 26 '69		
MAY 14 '69		
OCT 24 '75		
NOV 21 '75		
OCT 22 '75		
JAN 17 '76		
APR 7 '76		
MAR 9 '77		
APR 19 '78		
FEB 10 '82		
MAR 21 '84		
MAR 9 '88		